LOVE CLOUD

Kat Ramsburg

I0140059

BROADWAY PLAY PUBLISHING INC
New York
www.broadwayplaypublishing.com
info@broadwayplaypublishing.com

LOVE CLOUD
© Copyright 2020 Kat Ramsburg

First edition: November 2020
I S B N: 978-0-88145-881-7

Book design: Marie Donovan
Page make-up: Adobe InDesign
Typeface: Palatino

LOVE CLOUD was commissioned and produced by The Evergreen School in Shoreline, Washington, and was directed by Vanessa Miller.

CHARACTERS & SETTING

CLOUD*, *(genderless) keeper of all secrets. Only addresses the audience.*

THE KIDS:

DAX DIAMOND, *(M), just kicked out of the famous boy band, Love Cloud, for being too much of a troublemaker.*

KIMBERLY, *(F), obsessed with* DAX *and his former boy band.*

HUNTON, *(M), overdramatic and enthusiastic.* KIMBERLY'*s best friend.*

PIPPA, *(F), publishes the school gossip column.*

WINSTON, *(M),* PIPPA'*s lackey, but he has morals.*

CORDELIA, *(F), her real name is Janet, but no one knows that. She loves all things Shakespeare.*

JANE, *(F), people often forget she is in the room, which is fine with her.*

XASHA, *(F), Pronounced "Sasha." Her parents were trying to be clever, but brains don't run in the family.*

THE ADULTS:

MISS HOPE, *everyone's favorite teacher. She exudes warmth and understanding.*

MR STANTON, *the math teacher. Dreams of being a stand up comedian.*

ZEPHYR**, *(any gender)*, DAX's *personal assistant.*

PRINCIPAL SHEN**, *(any gender), Can also play a non-speaking student in earlier scenes.*

APPLE GENIUS**, *(any gender), Can also play a non-speaking student in earlier scenes.*

REPORTERS (any genders), *can be played by* MISS HOPE, MR STANTON, *and* APPLE GENIUS, *or other non-speaking students.*

*CLOUD *uses the "they" pronoun, as they are genderless.*

***For these roles, I've used female pronouns. If you cast a male or non-binary actor, please feel free to adjust to appropriate pronouns.*

Rutledge High School, Anytown U.S.A.

(The stage is flooded with sounds of text messages, instant messages, typing, pinging, sending, etc.)

(Characters appear in various positions around the stage. As it progresses, their lines overlap each other creating a cacophony of information.)

HUNTON: *(Texting)* O.M.G! I.D.K. L.O.L.
(Send)

JANE: *(On her laptop)* Anyone have the lab worksheet from O'Reilly's biology? 3rd period?
(Send)

PIPPA: *(Snap chatting)* Hey pretties! Keep an eye out for the next issue of Pippa's Ponderings, hitting your devices later today.
(Send)

KIMBERLY: *(Takes a selfie and posts it to Instagram)* I LOVE YOU LOVE CLOUD! Hashtag number one fan.
(Post)

JANE: *(On her laptop)* Hello? Anyone?
(Send)

WINSTON: *(Yik Yak)* Hey Cordelia.
(Send)

CORDELIA: *(Yik Yak)* "Away, you three inch fool!"
(Send)

XASHA: *(Into iPhone)* Siri, how come animals can talk on T V , but not in real life?

SIRI: (*Sound cue? Or off-stage voice*) I don't understand the question.

XASHA: (*Into iPhone*) AN-I-MALS. Talking ANIMALS!

(*Silence*)

CLOUD: Every day two-point-five quintillion bytes of data is produced. That's two-point-five followed by eighteen zeros! Emails, photos, Internet searches, online purchases, satellite images, etcetera. Two-point-five quintillion! And my job is to store it all. It's a dream job for a Type A like myself. Sorting, organizing, filing away. The most important part of my job is being able to recall information as soon as someone needs it.

MISS HOPE: (*Typing*) Seeking: Respectable gentleman friend.

MR STANTON: (*Typing*) Fantasy football stats.

CLOUD: I'm so Type A that even if you're certain you'll never need something again, I keep it. You may think it's gone, but I promise you, it isn't. Those photos you don't want anyone to see—got 'em! Hillary's emails—right here! The last voicemail from your dad before he died—definitely have that. Oh and that novel you've been writing since you were twenty but deleted on the night of your fortieth birthday because you decided that dream would never be realized—yup, I have it. (*To an adult in the audience*) Chapter six could use some tightening, but overall I'm hooked! (*Back to the audience*) And this is where we begin our story. I'm Cloud, and I'll be your narrator.
This is Kimberly.

KIMBERLY: (*Texting*) OMG! Did you see TMZ?

(*Send*)

CLOUD: And her best friend, Hunton.

(Ping)

HUNTON: *(Texting)* Ugh. No. Mom dragged me to yoga with her.

(Send)

(Ping)

KIMBERLY: *(Texting)* Dax is leaving Love Cloud!

CLOUD: Love Cloud is the BIGGEST boy band since One Direction. Or for you parents, since New Kids on the Block. And for you grandparents, The Beatles. And Kimberly is their number one fan.

KIMBERLY: *(Texting)* Emoji breaking heart
Emoji rain cloud
(Send)

(Ping)

HUNTON: *(Texting)*
OHMYGOSHAREYOUFREAKINGKIDDINGME?
Emoji fireworks
(Send)

(On another part of the stage)

CLOUD: This is Pippa. She takes a lot of selfies, and is the school gossip queen.

(PIPPA snaps a selfie.)

PIPPA: *(Blogging)* Hey pretties. Pippa here. Word on the street is that Dax Diamond was kicked out of the world famous boy band, Love Cloud. His bad boy behaviors proved too much for the band's wholesome image.

WINSTON: *(Over her shoulder)*
Wholesome is spelled W-H-O-L-E-Some.

PIPPA: I know that.

WINSTON: You spelled it without a W.

PIPPA: I wasn't finished.

CLOUD: That's Winston. Her trusty sidekick.

(Back to HUNTON *and* KIMBERLY, *who are now at school and reading* PIPPA's *blog on* KIMBERLY's *cell, or tablet.)*

HUNTON: How does she always have the inside scoop?

KIMBERLY: I'm pretty sure her dad is Edward Snowden.

HUNTON: For realsies?

*(*KIMBERLY *gasps.)*

HUNTON: What?

KIMBERLY: Look.
(She points back to the device.)

PIPPA: What to do with a boy band reject? Send him to finishing school of course. But with no finishing school in sight, Rutledge High School will have to do.

HUNTON & KIMBERLY:
DAXDIAMONDISCOMINGTORUTLEDGEHIGH!!!!!!

PIPPA: See you in chemistry, Dax. X-O-X-O, Pippa.

CLOUD: You're wondering how Dax Diamond got kicked out of Love Cloud, aren't you? It isn't for me to share his secrets. I'll just say, there are photos. And if you saw those photos…you would never eat ice cream again. He thought he deleted them, but as I've told you, *(Pointing to their head)* they're all right here. The problem is, someone hacked me and well…T M Z got them.

HUNTON & KIMBERLY:
OHMYGOSHOHMYGOSHOHMYGOSH!

*(*MISS HOPE *appears.)*

CLOUD: This is Miss Hope. She's a romantic through and through. Internet searches include, "Chicken Soup for the Lonely Soul," numerous viewings of "Love Actually," "Cute Kitten Videos," and compulsive visits to OneTrueLove dot com, where she has been searching for "The One" for five years.

MISS HOPE: Class, please take your seats.

(The students enter and sit.)

MISS HOPE: As you may have read in this morning's, "Pippa's Ponderings," we will have a new student starting today. Now, it's very important that we treat him like we would treat any other student at this school. Can someone remind me what our school values are?

(JANE raises her hand.)

MISS HOPE: Anyone? Surely someone knows.

(CORDELIA raises her hand.)

MISS HOPE: Yes, Cordelia.

CORDELIA: "Ignorance is the curse of God; knowledge is the wing wherewith we fly to heaven."

MISS HOPE: Henry VI, Act 4, Scene 7.

CORDELIA: Well done.

MISS HOPE: Thank you, but can you answer my question?

CORDELIA: Um…no.

(XASHA raises her hand.)

MISS HOPE: Yes. Sasha.

XASHA: Is Dax going to be here in person or as a hologram?

(KIMBERLY screams an ear piercing "Beatles mania" scream. HUNTON joins in, followed by many others in the class.)

MISS HOPE: Students! Students!

(The students calm down and reveal…DAX DIAMOND. The naughty boy of Love Cloud. He's part Harry Styles, part James Dean, and part Disney pop star.)

DAX: Hey. 'Sup?

MISS HOPE: You must be Dax. Welcome.

DAX: This is my assistant, Zephyr.

MISS HOPE: Oh! Welcome Zephyr.

ZEPHYR: We're going to need to do some rearranging in here. This room is *not* feng shui and Dax can *only* be in rooms that have been feng shui'd.

DAX: It's hereditary.

MISS HOPE: Of course, I totally understand.

(PIPPA *raises her hand.*)

PIPPA: Miss Hope?

MISS HOPE: Yes, Pippa.

PIPPA: Since Dax is starting the school year late, and will be behind on his classes, you should assign him a peer tutor. You know, a one-on-one kind of thing.

MISS HOPE: What a wonderful suggestion! Kimberly, you are the top student in my class. Would you mind being Dax's personal tutor?

PIPPA: Wait a minute!

KIMBERLY: I…uh…well…see…I…me…him…ugh… YES!!!!!!!!!!!!!!!!!!!!!

MISS HOPE: Perfect. Now everyone to study hall while Zephyr and I fang sweet the classroom.

(*The students file out.* PIPPA *and* WINSTON *give* KIMBERLY *the death glare.*)

(CORDELIA *approaches* MISS HOPE.)

CORDELIA: "I shall the effect of this good lesson keeps as watchman to my heart."

MISS HOPE: Hamlet, Act 1, Scene 3. That was easy.

*(*KIMBERLY *and* DAX *hang back.* DAX *turns on the charm. It works.)*

DAX: Hey.

KIMBERLY: Hey. I mean, hi. Hi. I'm Kimberly. You're Dax.

DAX: I know.

KIMBERLY: What am I saying? Of course you know. You get to wake up every day and say to yourself, "I'm Dax Diamond." What does that feel like?

DAX: Uh…

KIMBERLY: I bet it feels incredible. Like there's nothing in the entire world that you can't do. I, on the other hand, have to wake up every morning and say, "I'm Kimberly Flower." Then the sound of nothing follows. Did you know nothing has a sound? I didn't until I said my name out loud.

DAX: Your last name is flower? Like a plant?

KIMBERLY: Yeah. Flowers are of the plant division Magnoliophyta, also referred to as the Angiosperms.

DAX: So, like, what kind of flower are you?

KIMBERLY: Oh, um, I'm not—I don't know. Maybe a daisy? No! Wait, a lily! No! Wait, a—

DAX: I'd be the kind that eats people! That'd be so rad.

KIMBERLY: Um. A: That plant doesn't really exist outside of the musical, *Little Shop of Horrors,* and B: You want to be a cannibal?

DAX: What's that?

KIMBERLY: Someone who eats people.

DAX: Gross! No! If I was a *plant* I would eat people. But I wouldn't like, eat someone in real life. I'm vegan.

KIMBERLY: You are?

DAX: I mean I like burgers and chicken fingers, but like, I'm not really into meatloaf, so yeah.

KIMBERLY: Yeah, that's not what—have you gone to school, like, ever?

DAX: Zephyr handles the school end of things.

KIMBERLY: Zephyr does your homework?

DAX: Probably.

KIMBERLY: What about tests?

DAX: What's that?

KIMBERLY: OH MY GOSH, how are you even walking?

DAX: On my legs, duh.

KIMBERLY: It's a good thing you're handsome because—

DAX: You think I'm handsome?

KIMBERLY: Uh…I didn't mean…I just meant… Not like, *handsome*. Just like, you know…

DAX: Yeah. I know. *(He flashes his signature smile.)*

CLOUD: They say, never meet your heroes…
Uh oh. Incoming.

(The stage is flooded with sounds of text messages, instant messages, typing, pinging, sending, etc.)

HUNTON: *(Texting)* OHMYGOSHWHEREAREYOU TELLMEEVERYTHING!
(Send)

JANE: *(Texting)* Mom? Can you pick me up? I don't feel well.
(Send)

PIPPA: *(Snap chatting)* Hey pretties! Take it from me, Dax Diamond is just as handsome in person as you've imagined him to be.
(Send)

HUNTON: *(Texting)*
WHEREAREYOUI'MGOINGCRAZY!
(Send)

JANE: *(On her laptop)* It me. Jane. Your daughter?
(Send)

DAX: *(Texting)* Zephyr, I need you to carry my books to my next class.
(Send)

KIMBERLY: *(Texting)* Emjoi confused face.
(Send)

HUNTON: *(Texting)* What does that mean?
(Send)

WINSTON: *(Yik Yak)* Hey Cordelia. Dax seems kind of cool, right?
(Send)

CORDELIA: *(Yik Yak)* "Let no such man be trusted."
(Send)

XASHA: *(Into phone)* Siri, what's in mystery meat?

(All their phones ping at the same time.)

CLOUD: Now, you need to know that I didn't send the message the kids are about to receive, but it did technically go through me, and since it was anonymous, I'm going to have to say these lines. But it was not me! Are we clear on that?
Text Message: Word on the street is that Miss Kimberly Flower has made her mark on Dax Diamond. That didn't take long.

(All the students turn to look at KIMBERLY.)

KIMBERLY: Who sent this?

(Everyone disperses.)

HUNTON: Tell me everything!

KIMBERLY: There's nothing to tell. He's dumb. He's rude. He's not the Dax Diamond we know.

HUNTON: Maybe this is the *real* Dax Diamond.

KIMBERLY: If so, I can't have a crush on him anymore.

(HUNTON *and* KIMBERLY *head to their next class.*)

CLOUD: Young love. How quickly it fades. Kimberly goes home and deletes all of her Love Cloud fan fiction from her laptop. I read most of it. That girl could be the next J K Rowling, except, you know, accepting of the L G B T Q community. Which like, let's face it, Hermione was probably—
I'm off topic.

(MISS HOPE *and* MR STANTON *enter from opposite sides of the stage, engrossed in their phones, each unaware of the other.*)

MISS HOPE: (*Overlapping*) Doesn't like cats. No. Lives with his mom. No. Profile pic is *with* his mom. No.

MR STANTON: (*Overlapping*) Injured! No! Okay…let's see. Trade him and uh—

(MISS HOPE *and* MR STANTON *bump into each other.*)

MISS HOPE: Oh! Hello Mr Stanton.

MR STANTON: Miss Hope.

MISS HOPE: How's the math department today.

MR STANTON: Well, the geometry teacher is out.

MISS HOPE: Oh no! Why?

MR STANTON: She sprained her angle. (*Beat*) Her *angle*. As in a right *angle*.

MISS HOPE: Oh! Yes. I thought you said ankle.

MR STANTON: No. Angle. It was a math joke.

MISS HOPE: Yes. I understand now. Well, I should be off. We start *Watership Down* today.

MR STANTON: That's the one with the cute little bunnies, right?

MISS HOPE: …Yes.

MR STANTON: A book fell on my head once. I had no one to blame but my shelf. Get it? My shelf. Like a bookshelf.

MISS HOPE: Good day Mr. Stanton.

MR STANTON: Good day Miss Hope.

(MISS HOPE *exits one direction and* MR STANTON *exits the other.*)

CLOUD: I'm sure most of you are thinking, "Ah, that's the B Plot." It isn't. I just wanted to show you how many bad jokes can be found on the internet. Back to our story. The students were just heading to lunch when…

(The students fill the stage, one their way to lunch when, a cacophony of pings is heard.)

CLOUD: Text message: Poor little Winston. Not only is he Pippa's lackey, but he still wets the bed. Maybe that's why his crush on Cordelia will never amount to anything.

(All the students look at WINSTON.*)*

*(*WINSTON *looks at* CORDELIA.*)*

WINSTON: No I don't! Cordelia. I…I…

CORDELIA: "How wayward is this foolish love."

*(*CORDELIA *exists.* WINSTON *chases after her.*)*

WINSTON: I don't wet the bed! Well, not this month!

*(*KIMBERLY *approaches* PIPPA.*)*

KIMBERLY: Why are you doing this?

PIPPA: Doing what?

KIMBERLY: I do not have my claws in Dax, and what you just did to Winston was really mean.

PIPPA: You think I sent those texts?

HUNTON: Who else would it be?

PIPPA: I don't know, but it's not me. I have better things to do than gossip about nobodies like you and Winston.

(PIPPA *turns to leave but sees* JANE.)

PIPPA: You. Are you new here?

JANE: We've been in school together since Kindergarten.

PIPPA: Great. You're my new Winston. Come along Winston.

JANE: It's Jane, actually.

PIPPA: Whatever Winston.

(PIPPA *and* JANE *leave.* XASHA *trails behind.*)

XASHA: I'm so sorry Winston! I've been calling you Jane all these years.

(DAX *approaches* HUNTON *and* KIMBERLY. ZEPHYR *is close behind.*)

DAX: So this is what I've been missing out on by not going to school?

KIMBERLY: It's not normally like this. Someone is just trying to cause drama.

HUNTON: We haven't officially met. I'm Hunton. Kimberly's B F F.

DAX: B F F?

HUNTON: Best friend forever.

DAX: Oh. That's a thing?

HUNTON: Uh, yeah.

(DAX *turns to* ZEPHYR*.*)

DAX: Zephyr, you're my B F F.

ZEPHYR: As long as those checks keep clearing.

DAX: So what now?

KIMBERLY: Now we eat lunch.

DAX: Where's catering?

HUNTON: In the cafeteria.

DAX: *(To* ZEPHYR*)* You made sure to call ahead?

ZEPHYR: I did but they don't offer gluten free, or dairy free here. And it's a health violation to bring in your own chef.

DAX: What am I supposed to eat?!

HUNTON: Well, it's pizza day so—

DAX: I *love* pizza!

(The foursome exits to lunch.)

CLOUD: Who could be sending those text messages? Will Miss Hope find love? Will Dax realize that pizza isn't gluten or dairy free? The suspense is killing me! Which means it's time to turn our attention to one of our underdeveloped characters, Xasha. As you might have noticed, Xasha is a product of the generation who hasn't had to commit anything to memory because her good friend Siri is always by her side. Here are some of Xasha's greatest hits.

*(*XASHA *enters, stands center, pulls out her phone.)*

XASHA: Siri, what do you call a male ladybug?
Siri, do bees have knees?
Siri, can cows be lactose intolerant?
Siri, what is the speed of dark?
(Then, hushed)
Siri, can my cat read my mind?

CLOUD: Some would call her dim. Others would call her curious. More on that later. Time for math class!

(MR STANTON *and the students fill the stage.*)

MR STANTON: What did the little mermaid wear to math class?

(*The kids stare at him with blank expressions.*)

MR STANTON: An algebra.

(*The kids groan.*)

MR STANTON: All right. All right. Open your books to chapter seven.

(*A cacophony of pings*)

MR STANTON: No phones in the classroom! How many times do I have to—

CLOUD: Text message: It seems one Mr Stanton and one Miss Hope were caught canoodling in the teachers lounge at lunch.

STUDENTS: Ewwww.

(MR STANTON *grabs one of the kid's phones and reads it.*)

MR STANTON: This is categorically untrue! We were in the teachers lounge. But we—she was over there. And I was over there. Who would spread such a vicious rumor? Class dismissed!

(MR STANTON *runs out of the classroom.*)

KIMBERLY: We've got to get to the bottom of this! Someone in this room is causing drama and it has to stop!

(*The phones ping again.*)

CLOUD: Text: Want to read something juicy? Here's a link to Kimberly Flower's Love Cloud Fan Fiction.

KIMBERLY: Wait a minute! Everyone delete that. Hunton, grab everyone's phones.

PIPPA: *(Overdramatic reading)* "Dax took Kim behind the bleachers at lunch. She was nervous. He was nervous. Would their first kiss be—"

KIMBERLY: Stop! Please!

DAX: *(Regarding what he's reading)* Oh. Wow. Yeah. Not usually my move, but…I could try that.

KIMBERLY: It was just silly fun.

PIPPA: I'm surprised you have enough time for homework with… *(Scrolling forever)* forty-three chapters of fan fic!

JANE: I think it's pretty good.

CORDELIA: It's not Shakespeare, but it's better than Raleigh so…

WINSTON: I don't wet the bed!

XASHA: We know, Jane.

(KIMBERLY approaches PIPPA.)

KIMBERLY: This proves it's not me. What about you, Pippa? You're the only one who has made it through unscathed.

PIPPA: Untrue. Xasha and Hunton have yet to be unmasked. Though truth be told, I'm not sure Xasha has the bandwidth to keep a secret. Hunton though… *(To HUNTON)* What's hiding in your closet?

HUNTON: Mostly Tom Ford and Steve McQueen. It's an addiction. What can I say?

PIPPA: Well I'm an open book, so whichever one of you is playing Julian Assange, good luck finding anything on me. *(Beat)* Come on Winston. You can watch me get a facial.

(JANE and WINSTON both stand. They look at each other, then to PIPPA. Which one was she talking to?)

PIPPA: *(Pointing to JANE)* That one. Let's go.

(JANE *follows* PIPPA *out.* WINSTON *slumps in his seat. He never liked being* PIPPA's *lackey, but he's lost without her.*)

KIMBERLY: If it's no one in this room, do you think it's one of the teachers? Or the Principal?

HUNTON: Why would the teachers care about high school drama?

WINSTON: Maybe they're trying to teach us a lesson about social media and how everything we put online is there forever?

CORDELIA: They don't even know how to put their phones on Airplane mode.

WINSTON: Good point.

HUNTON: So what are we going to do?

XASHA: Siri, who is telling our secrets?

SIRI: "There are no secrets that time does not reveal."

DAX: Dang. Siri got deep for a second.

(*The students turn to* DAX...*why had they not thought of him?*)

HUNTON: It's you! You're the one doing this.

DAX: Me? No way. I don't know anything about you guys.

CORDELIA: But you like to cause trouble for people.

DAX: Sure, but—

WINSTON: And we didn't have any of this drama until you got here.

DAX: Unlucky coincidence.

KIMBERLY: Is it?

DAX: Yeah.

XASHA: Siri, is Dax Diamond telling our secrets?

SIRI: Dax Diamond secrets. Here are some photos I found.

(DAX *grabs* XASHA's *phone.*)

DAX: Whoa! Whoa! It's not me, okay. I give you my word.

WINSTON: I'm going to interview the Principal and see if she has any information.

CORDELIA: I'll go with you.

WINSTON: You will?

CORDELIA: "It is not in the stars to hold our destiny, but in ourselves."

WINSTON: Cool.

(CORDELIA *and* WINSTON *exit.*)

KIMBERLY: Hunton and Xasha, you go interview Mr. Stanton and Miss Hope and see who else was in the teachers lounge with them.

XASHA: Mr. Stanton is so funny!

HUNTON: What are you going to do?

KIMBERLY: First I'm going to change the password on my Dropbox account, and then I'm going to figure out the phone number that is sending these text messages.

DAX: And I'm going to help her!

KIMBERLY: You know about computers?

DAX: My dream job is to be an Apple Genius, because I love apples, and it would be cool to be a genius.

KIMBERLY: Uh huh…

HUNTON: Okay, text if you need anything.

(HUNTON *and* XASHA *exit.*)

ZEPHYR: I'm going to go figure out where your helicopter can land for after school pick ups. We might

need to remove that protected forest behind the school
to create a secure landing site.

(ZEPHYR *exits.* DAX *and* KIMBERLY *are left alone.*)

DAX: That was some pretty sweet fan fic.

KIMBERLY: I wrote it years ago.

DAX: It's dated yesterday.

KIMBERLY: It's private!

DAX: I'm just saying, I think it's sweet.

KIMBERLY: Yeah, well that was before I met you.

DAX: What do you mean?

KIMBERLY: Have you looked in the mirror lately, Dax.

DAX: Several times a day, actually.

KIMBERLY: It's a metaphor.

DAX: A what?

KIMBERLY: You're sixteen years old. It's time to learn
how to be a normal person.

DAX: I'm in school. I ate whatever that was they put on
my tray at lunch. How much more normal do I need to
be?

KIMBERLY: Your personal assistant is chopping down a
forest so your helicopter can have a parking spot.

DAX: Zephyr's the best. Worth every penny.

KIMBERLY: You're missing the point.

DAX: Okay, look. I can't ride the school bus, or the bus
will be chased by paparazzi, which will be unsafe for
the other students. I can't bring my own lunch or it will
look like I think I'm too good to eat what the rest of
you eat, even though whatever I just ate is giving me
the worst stomach ache I've had in years.

KIMBERLY: And the reason you can't do your own homework?

DAX: I get it. I'm spoiled, or privileged—whatever you want to call it. But I'm here, and I'm trying to fit in. And it would be really nice, if you gave me the benefit of the doubt for five minutes.

(DAX *and* KIMBERLY'*s phones ping.*)

DAX: See! How could I have sent that while I was standing here talking to you?

CLOUD: Text message: Turns out Cordelia Hathaway's name is really Janet Krankenputz. She lives on a farm, and castrates cows for fun.

DAX: We've got to figure out who is doing this. Let's go.

(DAX *and* KIMBERLY *start out the door, but she stops.*)

KIMBERLY: Dax? I'm sorry I judged you.

DAX: I'm sorry I'm not the Dax Diamond, the music industry made me out to be.

KIMBERLY: For what it's worth, this Dax Diamond is way better.

(DAX *and* KIMBERLY *exit.*)

CLOUD: See what can happen when we put down our devices and actually talk to each other? So it turns out that Dax isn't as bad of a boy as he pretends to be, and Kimberly's fan fiction shouldn't be a source of embarrassment.

Meanwhile, in another part of the school…

(CORDELIA *and* WINSTON *interrogate* PRINCIPAL SHEN.)

WINSTON: Where were you during first period?

PRINCIPAL SHEN: Here in my office.

CORDELIA: Do you have any electronic devices?

PRINCIPAL SHEN: My desktop for work. My iPad for meetings. My iPod for when I jog. My blackberry for personal phone calls.

WINSTON: A blackberry?

PRINCIPAL SHEN: Yes?

CORDELIA: Psst!

(CORDELIA *and* WINSTON *huddle together.*)

CORDELIA: *(Hushed)* It's unlikely that someone who uses a blackberry would know how to hack personal data systems, and anonymously send text messages.

WINSTON: Good point. *(He turns back to* PRINCIPAL SHEN.*)* Principal Shen. What is your iCloud password?

PRINCIPAL SHEN: MisterMittens123

CORDELIA: MisterMittens123, you say?

PRINCIPAL SHEN: He is the best cat.

WINSTON: Psst!

(CORDELIA *and* WINSTON *huddle together.*)

WINSTON: *(Hushed)* I don't think Principal Shen is our gal.

CORDELIA: I concur. But this is too much fun to stop now.

(CORDELIA *turns back to* PRINCIPAL SHEN.*)*

CORDELIA: Principal Shen, we are now going to administer the following Buzzfeed Quiz and you are going to find out which Hogwarts House you would be sorted into.

One. Pick a candy: Fizzy Wizzy, Bertie Bott's…

(WINSTON, CORDELIA, *and* PRINCIPAL SHEN *fade away.*)

CLOUD: And in another part of the school…

(MISS HOPE, MR STANTON, HUNTON *and* XASHA *appear.*)

MISS HOPE: I don't know who would spread this rumor.

HUNTON: You didn't see anyone unusual in the teachers lounge?

MR STANTON: Just the usual people. Teachers heating up leftovers, administrators getting a soda from the vending machine.

XASHA: Very curious.

HUNTON: Why is that curious?

XASHA: I just googled "how to be a detective," and it said to be very curious, so I'm being very curious.

HUNTON: *(To MISS HOPE and MR STANTON)* Is there any truth to the rumor?

MR STANTON: Young man!

HUNTON: I don't need details, but we have to figure out if the secrets being revealed are truth or lies.

MISS HOPE: I would never canoodle with—I mean, not on school grounds!

HUNTON: But you would canoodle, *off* school grounds?

(MISS HOPE and MR STANTON share an awkward, embarrassed glance.)

XASHA: Very curious.

(Their phones ping.)

CLOUD: Text message: She plays dumb, but Xasha's actually a certified genius. She's Mensa's member of the month. Next time you've got a test, better cozy up to Xasha.

HUNTON: Okay, so now we know the secrets are lies.

(MISS HOPE and MR STANTON look to XASHA.)

MISS HOPE: I'm sorry, Xasha. We tried to keep your secret.

HUNTON: Wait. This secret is *true?*

(Beat)

XASHA: Fine. Yes. I'm a genius. Big whoop. I already graduated from Yale Law, and Harvard Medical, but I wanted the normal high school experience so I'm here. Is it a crime to actually *like* high school?

MR STANTON: *(To* HUNTON*)* She writes all of my lesson plans. It gives me more time to work on my stand up comedy. Speaking of which, why don't math teachers drink? Because it's wrong to drink and derive.

CLOUD: Obviously, the kids were getting nowhere with their investigation, and the casualties were piling up. Principal Shen learned she is a Hufflepuff, while Winston and Cordelia learned they make a great team.

*(*WINSTON *and* CORDELIA *leave* PRINCIPAL SHEN'*s office, quite pleased with themselves.)*

CORDELIA: Even though we're no closer finding out who the hacker is, that was fun.

WINSTON: We should do that again sometime.

CORDELIA: Totally. Well, see ya.

WINSTON: See ya.

(They both go their separate ways.)

CLOUD: Incoming.

Google search: "Shakespeare quotes."

*(*WINSTON *turns around suddenly…)*

WINSTON: Janet Krankenputz!

*(*CORDELIA *turns to face him.)*

WINSTON: "What's in a name? That which we call a rose by any other name would smell as sweet."

CORDELIA: Winston?

WINSTON: "Hear my soul speak. Of the very instant that I saw you, did my heart fly at your service"

(CORDELIA *doesn't believe what she's hearing.*)

WINSTON: "Doubt thou the stars are fire, doubt that the sun doth move. Doubt truth to be a liar, but never doubt that I love."

CORDELIA: "Speak low, if you speak of love."

WINSTON: *(Whispering)* "I love you more than words can wield the matter."

(CORDELIA *and* WINSTON *embrace.*)

CLOUD: And *that*, ladies and gentlemen, is our B-plot.

(CORDELIA *and* WINSTON *run off together.*)

CLOUD: Back to the A-plot. Who is sending these anonymous text messages? And where have Pippa and Jane been? Utilizing the locations app on her iPhone, I've been tracking Pippa's every move:
First stop: Krispy Kreme

(JANE *holds a box of Krispy Kreme while* PIPPA *eats and takes selfies.*)

CLOUD: Second stop: Bliss Beauty Spa

(JANE *paints* PIPPA's *nails while* PIPPA *takes selfies.*)

CLOUD: Third stop: Forever 21

(JANE *holds a pile of clothes while* PIPPA *takes selfies.*)

CLOUD: Fourth stop…oh, interesting. The Apple Store.

(*An* APPLE GENIUS *appears.*)

APPLE GENIUS: How can I help you today?

PIPPA: Someone at my school is hacking into people's clouds and revealing secrets. I need you to make sure my phone is impenetrable.

APPLE GENIUS: Nothing is truly impenetrable.

PIPPA: But there has to be *something* you can do.

APPLE GENIUS: Why? Are you hiding something?

PIPPA: No! It's just no one's business what I keep in my cloud.

APPLE GENIUS: But if you're not hiding anything, then there's nothing to worry about.

PIPPA: Have you turned on the news lately? Do you understand how this world works?

APPLE GENIUS: I don't watch T V actually. It rots the brain.

PIPPA: Let me guess, you own lots of books.

APPLE GENIUS: I do!

PIPPA: And a couple of ferrets.

APPLE GENIUS: Uh…no?

PIPPA: Here's the deal. I'm only fifteen but I fully plan on attending Vassar, where I will get my poly sci degree before attending Harvard for my law degree, which will come in handy when I run for state office, then work my way up into the White House where I will eventually become President. I don't need a silly photo or an off handed comment coming back to haunt me, from the years when my underdeveloped amygdala was making decisions. Do you understand what I'm saying?

APPLE GENIUS: Not really.

PIPPA: I need this phone to secure!

APPLE GENIUS: But as I've explained, that's virtually impossible. There's really only one way to make sure that nothing gets out there that you don't want out there.

PIPPA: Great. Let's do that!

(JANE *takes* PIPPA'*s phone and smashes it, by stomping on it.*)

PIPPA: My phone! My beautiful phone!

APPLE GENIUS: Woah. I didn't see you standing there.

JANE: Story of my life.

APPLE GENIUS: Are you looking for a job by chance?

(JANE'*s phone pings.* PIPPA'*s makes a pathetic sound.*)

CLOUD: Text message: Did you know our dear Hunton is a figure skater? His long program is performed to the theme music from *Twilight*. Click here for video.

(KIMBERLY *runs into* HUNTON *in the hallway. They've both just received the text.* DAX *is close behind.*)

KIMBERLY: Hunton! This is nothing to be embarrassed by.

HUNTON: Who said I'm embarrassed? I'm proud of it.

KIMBERLY: But you never told me. I would have come and cheered you on!

HUNTON: You have better things to do with your weekends.

KIMBERLY: You're my *best* friend. Best friends go watch their best friend figure skate, dressed like a vampire… in tights.

HUNTON: Okay, okay, you can come! Saturday. Eleven A M. Ice King skate rink.

KIMBERLY: I'll be the one wearing garlic.

DAX: Maybe I can come too?

(HUNTON *looks to* KIMBERLY.)

HUNTON: Do we like him again?

KIMBERLY: We are giving him a second chance.

DAX: I'm going to work on being a normal guy. Normal guys watch ice skating, right?

HUNTON: It's their favorite sport.

(CORDELIA *and* WINSTON *enter.*)

CORDELIA: Okay, it's definitely not Principal Shen.

KIMBERLY: Where have you two been?

CORDELIA: Um…nowhere.

WINSTON: Okay, by my calculations the only person who has yet to be outed in Pippa. If that doesn't incriminate her, I don't know what does!

(PIPPA *has entered, with* JANE *close behind. She holds out a ziplock bag with the bits and pieces of her broken phone.*)

PIPPA: How about this for proof it's not me?

HUNTON: What happened?

PIPPA: Winston happened.

JANE: She means me.

XASHA: I can fix it.
(*She takes the bag.*)

PIPPA: It's our resident genius. Really pulled one over on us, didn't you?

XASHA: You decided I was stupid because I ask a lot of questions. I'm sorry if my brain is naturally curious and has the ability to take in more information than yours.

(*As if by magic [and sleight of hand],* XASHA *hands* PIPPA *her fully restored phone.*)

JANE: Woah.

PIPPA: There's no way this works.

(*But the phone pings. Followed by a ping on everyone else's phones.*)

CLOUD: Text message: One last victim. Dax Diamond. You didn't think you were going to be able to hide in plain sight, did you? Every news outlet in the city has been notified of your whereabouts. Get ready.

(ZEPHYR *is heard off stage.*)

ZEPHYR: *(O S)* Wait! Stop!

(ZEPHYR *enters fending off* REPORTERS *who follow close behind.*)

REPORTERS: *(Shouting over each other.)*

Dax! Dax Diamond! Can I just get a quote! Etc.

REPORTER 1: What's it like being normal?

REPORTER 2: Have you been suspended yet?

REPORTER 3: Are you going to go solo now that Love Cloud kicked you out?

ZEPHYR: Dax has no comment!

REPORTER 1: We want to hear from him.

DAX: It's okay Zephyr. Thanks for trying.

REPORTER 1: What's it like being normal?

DAX: If by being normal, you mean that a bunch of reporters show up at your school…it's going well.

REPORTER 2: You always were a charmer. So, have you been suspended yet?

DAX: Not yet, but it's only my first day.

(PRINCIPAL SHEN *runs on stage.*)

PRINCIPAL SHEN: I'm so sorry Dax! These reporters should never have been on campus.

ZEPHYR: Exactly what I was saying.

PRINCIPAL SHEN: You'll have to leave right away.

(PRINCIPAL SHEN *and* ZEPHYR *try to herd the* REPORTERS *off, but* REPORTER 3 *gets away.*)

REPORTER 3: What about a solo career? Love Cloud has thirty-one million Instagram followers. Surely many of your fans would follow you.

(DAX *looks to* KIMBERLY.)

DAX: Actually, I think I'm going to try my hand at obscurity for a while. So far, I like it.

PRINCIPAL SHEN: Okay, time to go.

REPORTER 3: Obscurity? Is this some kind of publicity stunt?

REPORTERS 1 & 2: Yeah? What's going on? *(Etc)*

ZEPHYR: It's time to go!

DAX: Wait. What do you mean?

REPORTER 1: We got an "anonymous" tip that you were going to school here, but a quick internet search linked the email to an I.P. address registered to your assistant.

ZEPHYR: What? I would never!

DAX: Zephyr? You've been the one sending the text messages? What did these people ever do to you?

ZEPHYR: Nothing! They didn't do anything. Because *nothing happens at this school!* I'm bored. I'm used to the exciting life we used to live. I'm not used to being the assistant to a nobody. I was made to assist *famous people*. It's who I am! I don't do normal.

DAX: Zephyr, your fired.

ZEPHYR: But...but...I've been with you for *years*. This school is a temporary situation. Once your solo album drops you'll be famous again and I —

DAX: There is no solo album Zeph. There's 10th grade. Then 11th. Then college.

KIMBERLY: *(Whispers)* 12th grade.

DAX: 12th grade? Are you serious!? I have to do this for three years?

KIMBERLY: Yeah. Are you still interested?

DAX: I'm definitely interested. *(Beat. To* ZEPHYR.*)* Sorry Zephyr, you are no longer my assistant, or my best friend. I wish you well.

*(*ZEPHYR *exits, followed by the* REPORTERS.*)*

*(*DAX *turns to* KIMBERLY.*)*

DAX: I guess I'm in the market for a new B F F.

*(*HUNTON *steps between them.)*

HUNTON: Oh no. Hands off.

DAX: All right. Calm down She's all yours.

KIMBERLY: But you can sit with me at all of Hunton's figure skating competitions!

CLOUD: As Cordelia would often quote, all's well that ends well. Everyone changed their passwords, and updated their security settings on electric devices. Xasha decided she was above high school and decided to pursue a double Phd at M I T.

XASHA: Siri, what is the acceleration of a raindrop? *(She exits.)*

CLOUD: Cordelia and Winston went on to perform the leads in every play and musical presented at Rutledge High School. After college they joined a traveling Shakespeare troupe, Bard in the Yard, who performs Shakespeare in prison yards.

*(*CORDELIA *and* WINSTON *step forward.)*

WINSTON: *(As Benedict)* By my sword, Beatrice, thou lovest me.

CORDELIA: *(As Beatrice)* Do not swear it, and eat it.

WINSTON: I will swear by it that you love me, and I will make him eat it that says I love you not.

CORDELIA: Will you not eat your word?

WINSTON: With no sauce that can be devised to it. I protest I love thee.

CORDELIA: Why then, God forgive me.

WINSTON: What offence, sweet Beatrice?

CORDELIA: You have stayed me in a happy hour. I was about to protest I loved you.

(All the remaining actors on stage applaud. CORDELIA *and* WINSTON *bow and exit.)*

CLOUD: Hunton won silver in the Winter Olympics. He thought about going for gold but—

*(*HUNTON *steps forward with his silver medal.)*

HUNTON: It's clashes with my skin tone. I'm a winter. *(He kisses his medal and exits.)*

CLOUD: Pippa did go on to Vassar, and Harvard, became Mayor, then Governor, then Senator.

*(*PIPPA *steps forward.)*

PIPPA: Told you.

CLOUD: She was well on her way to the Presidency when an unfortunate photo scandal involving sorority hazing, a platypus, and some blue hair dye came to light.

PIPPA: Whatever. Now I run a multi-billion dollar hedge fund and have more money than I know what to do with. And Winston is still my assistant.

JANE: I changed my name. It seemed easier.

*(*PIPPA *exits,* JANE *follows.)*

CLOUD: And what of our lovers?

(DAX *and* KIMBERLY *step forward.*)

DAX & KIMBERLY: (*Talking over each other*) Oh, we're not together. We're just friends. *Good* friends. Etc.

CLOUD: I'm not talking about you guys. I'm talking about them.

(MISS HOPE *and* MR STANTON *appear.*)

MR STANTON: Two satellites decided to get married. The wedding wasn't much, but the reception was terrific.

(MISS HOPE *genuinely finds this funny.*)

MISS HOPE: Isn't he hilarious?

CLOUD: They married shortly after he wrote that joke. Mr. Stanton would eventually retire to pursue his comedy career full time. Miss Hope, everyone's favorite teacher, is still at Rutledge High. She has deleted all dating apps from her phone.

(MISS HOPE *and* MR STANTON *run off together.*)

(CLOUD *gestures to* DAX *and* KIMBERLY *that they can now step forward.*)

CLOUD: Dax did go on to a prosperous solo career, but not until he finished high school and learned how to be normal. Kimberly is a celebrated Young Adult author whose most recent best seller has been optioned by Netflix. Her first kiss *did* happen behind the bleachers, and it *was* with Dax, but it was then that she realized she would rather be under the bleachers with Ariana Grande than Dax Diamond. They remain good friends.

(KIMBERLY *shrugs and walks off.* DAX *gives his classic smile and head nod and exits.*)

CLOUD: Well, that about wraps things up. It's time to turn your phones back on and see how many of the two hundred thousand text messages sent per second, were sent to you. I hope you think of me every time you use Skype, or talk to Siri, or save a photo, or write an email, because you can be sure, I'll be thinking of you.

Thank you for coming. We'll see you next year!

(They walk off stage, waving.)

END OF PLAY

www.ingramcontent.com/pod-product-compliance
Lightning Source LLC
Chambersburg PA
CBHW070036110426
42741CB00035B/2794